The Incarnation of Christ

The Incarnation of Christ

A Spiritual Embryology

Pearl Goodwin

Floris Books

First published by Floris Books in 2026

© 2026 Pearl Goodwin
Pearl Goodwin has asserted her right under the
Copyright, Design and Patents Act 1988
to be identified as the Author of this Work

All rights reserved. No part of this book may be
reproduced in any form without written permission of
Floris Books, Edinburgh
www.florisbooks.co.uk

 Also available as an eBook

Authorised EU Representative: Easy Access System Europe,
Mustamae tee 50, 10621 Tallinn, Estonia
gpsr.requests@easproject.com

British Library CIP Data available
ISBN 978-178250-992-9

Contents

Foreword *by Peter Selg*	7
Introduction	11
The starting point	13
Biological Conception	19
Germ cell development	21
Conception	24
The third element	25
Further development of the embryo	30
Christological Embryology	37
The birth in the Gospel of Matthew	39
The birth in the Gospel of Luke	44
The spiritual background to the Matthew story	48
The spiritual background to the Luke story	50
The twelve-year-old in the temple	57
The spiritual background to the temple story	60
The lost eighteen years	67
Jesus' conversation with Mary	71
The Baptism by John	77

The Two Embryologies	83
The essential difference between the two embryologies	*83*
The Resurrection Body	*85*
The process of identification and the Resurrection	*87*
It is one embryology, not two	*94*
Birth in the Gospel of John	*96*
Conclusion	*99*
Notes	*101*
Bibliography	*102*
Acknowledgements	*103*

Foreword

> The biological or organic has an essential spiritual
> component, and the spiritual has an essential earthly
> component. Both are expressions of a reality that is
> a fundamental gesture of the cosmos that embraces
> heaven and earth. (From the Introduction. p. 17)

In his lecture cycle *The Fifth Gospel,* which he held in Oslo in 1913, Rudolf Steiner drew a series of remarkable comparisons between the life of Christ and an ordinary human life. He said the Baptism in the Jordan, when the divine Christ incarnated in the human Jesus of Nazareth, could be likened to human conception; the three years from Baptism to crucifixion with the development in the womb, and the death on Golgotha with human birth. He compared the forty days in between Golgotha and Ascension to a single human lifetime, and the events from Ascension to Pentecost with the subsequent transition of the human spirit-soul into the world of the spirit (see lecture of October 3, 1913). Such an approach to the life of Christ Jesus requires us to completely rethink almost everything that has been thought and felt in this regard, but it also opens up completely new and unexpected perspectives.

As a trained embryologist, geneticist and priest of the Christian Community, Pearl Goodwin is uniquely placed with her knowledge and skills. She is primarily, though by no means exclusively, concerned with Steiner's first comparison: the parallels that exist between biological conception and the Baptism in the Jordan, which was the spiritual conception of Christ in the body of Jesus of Nazareth. The author does not begin her exposition with the words 'Today I have begotten you' (Lk 3:22), but rather with a fascinating description of what today's embryology has to say about the union of the egg and sperm cell, thus beginning with the phenomena of biological conception. The polarity of the male and female reproductive cells, the 'two becoming one' and the chaos that occurs in the fertilised egg that allows for the entry of a third and higher principle, are described as stages of both biological and spiritual embryology. The descriptions given in the Matthew and Luke gospels of the birth of Jesus are also described in terms of a polarity, with the 'two becoming one' taking place in the Temple in Jerusalem in the twelfth year of Jesus's life. The embryological convulsions that occur in the first eighteen days are comparable to the spiritual convulsions of Jesus of Nazareth in the subsequent eighteen years of his life until the Baptism in the Jordan. The author shows the characteristics of the stages in the process of becoming are comparable and illuminate each other.

The 'conception' of the Christ being in Jesus of Nazareth at the time of the Baptism in the Jordan marks the beginning of a development that not only led to the missionary activity of Christ Jesus on earth, but also to a new corporeality, a new body that was destined for resurrection. The 'embryology' that Rudolf Steiner saw in the three years and the subsequent 'birth' through the death on Golgotha referred to this mysterious Resurrection Body. The aim of Pearl Goodwin's study is to provide a framework for understanding this body. As she states, 'The embryological approach becomes a way to approach the mystery' (p. 85).

Most impressive of all, Pearl describes how we fashion the spirit germ of our physical body during the cosmic Midnight Hour between death and a new birth. In that moment we experience the body fully from within and participate in the formation of each organ; there is a creative union – or even 'communion' – of centre and periphery, of 'I' and cosmos. What is fashioned anew in cosmic heights for every incarnating human being, occurred uniquely on earth in the formation of the Resurrection Body through the union of the Christ-spirit with the body of Jesus of Nazareth.

While this study deals with deep connections (even 'mysteries') that are difficult to understand, nevertheless it provides a lively introduction to the principles of development and to the realities that are at stake here. The descriptions in the book are as vivid as they are precise, and it becomes clear, as the author herself emphasises towards the end, that this is ultimately about one embryology not two. It is about a great span of development that embraces heaven and earth through the eternal activity of the Logos.

Ever since I met Pearl in Vancouver, Canada in 2008 and heard her first lectures on embryology, I hoped for a book from her and repeatedly asked her to write down her discoveries and points of view, which she also shared with us in conversation. It is a great pleasure that she has finally put pen to paper and that this book can be published.

Peter Selg
August 2025

Introduction

This study attempts to bring together two fields of knowledge that are not normally seen as belonging with each other. One is the conception and development of the child in the womb, which leads to a new embodiment of a human soul on the earth. The other is the 'conception' of the being of Christ in the body of Jesus of Nazareth at the Baptism in the Jordan. This is usually called the Incarnation.

Both realms, the biological and the spiritual, are approached using what is known as the Goethean method, that is, the development of ideas and thoughts through observation, rather than bringing already conceived ideas to the observation. The continual growth and metamorphosis of form in early embryology cannot easily be observed; in fact, the entire embryological development of the child is hidden in the womb of the mother. Microscopes and other scientific procedures are needed to make these early stages visible, and even then, only in books. However, what is shown in books can be objectively observed, always keeping in mind how they have been made.

Goethean observation can also be applied to the spiritual realm. This study relies heavily on the observation and knowledge of Rudolf Steiner and his ability to see into the worlds of spirit. He saw what most of us cannot see, but because of the trustworthiness of his methods and his person he allows us to 'see' that world and to work with these observations as facts in a Goethean way. The spiritual world becomes a field of observation that can give us thoughts, even new ones. So, in this study, both the visible and the invisible can be taken as fields of accurate observation, out of which thoughts can emerge that are true and are not simply fantasy. Biological embryology gains knowledge through the senses and instruments that enhance the senses. Spiritual embryology gains knowledge through trusted supersensible observation. The two together can bring a new unity of understanding.

One can never prove the spiritual by means of the empirical. Empirical methods show their trustworthiness by being repeatable, meaning an experiment or observation can be carried out by anyone, assuming they are suitably qualified, and the same results will be achieved each time. Such investigations take place in 'clock' time, what the Greeks called *chronos*, which refers to linear, measurable time. Spiritual investigation, however, needs a different quality of time, a moment when the spiritual and the earthly can meet. The Greeks called this qualitative aspect of time *kairos*. It refers to a particular moment of clock time and what happens within it tends to be unique. There are many examples of this kind of time and they are often experienced as destiny moments: for instance, when two people meet, or the moment of birth or death when the laws of the spirit meet and unite with the law of the earth. These moments are rarely repeatable in the empirical sense. However, through a rigorous process of development that drew upon the methods of natural science, Rudolf Steiner was able to check his spiritual findings and thereby place a kind of earthly method into the spiritual realm. That is one of the unique characteristics of his spiritual investigation, which is why it is called a spiritual science.

This study assumes a basic acceptance of the work of Rudolf Steiner. Many of the fundamentals of anthroposophy will be taken for granted.

The starting point

In the lecture cycle *The Fifth Gospel,* Rudolf Steiner spoke in a particular way about the Baptism in the Jordan when the being of Christ incarnated into the bodily sheaths of Jesus of Nazareth:

> The event ... called the Baptism by John ... relates to the life of the Christ as conception does to the life of a human being on earth. The life of Christ from then until the Mystery of Golgotha may be compared to the life of the embryo in its mother's womb. The Christ spirit may be said to have gone through embryonic life between the Baptism by John and the Mystery of Golgotha. The Mystery of Golgotha itself, that is, the death of Jesus, has to be seen as the birth of the Christ spirit on earth, whose real life on earth began after the Mystery of Golgotha. Then Christ went about with the Apostles who were in an altered state of consciousness at the time. Ascension and the pouring out of the spirit which followed must be seen as something which in our case would normally be regarded as entering into the world of spirit as we die.[1]

The Fifth Gospel is the only place where Rudolf Steiner described the incarnation in this way. We should say 'stated' rather than 'described' because he offers no details that explain the nature of this higher embryology in terms of ordinary human embryology. All that can be said for sure at this point is that both result in a body: in one a human body, in the other the Resurrection Body.

INTRODUCTION

This study is an attempt to gain some understanding of the spiritual conception through the phenomena of human conception. Both of these can be regarded as a step in incarnation, but taking place in different realms.

The word 'incarnation' is the anchor point of Rudolf Steiner's Christology. It comes from the Latin *in carne*, meaning, to enter flesh. This immediately tells us of a dynamic that is not part of modern thinking – that human beings, indeed all sentient beings, consist of interweaving parts that are separate from each other and must be brought together by this dynamic of 'incarnation'. There is a separation of conscious and unconscious, of body and soul/spirit. How they come together is the process of incarnation.

This is fundamental to all human life. Falling asleep at night is not simply the brain shutting down. It is something leaving the brain that allows it to shut down. That 'something', our awake consciousness is then able to return to its own home in the spirit and return again in the morning, renewed and refreshed. This is called 'waking up' and is the dynamic of incarnation on its smallest scale, the rhythm of day and night.

How our particular consciousness comes to be in our particular body belongs to the next level of incarnation, the rhythm of life and death. This is the content of an anthroposophically inspired embryology, which is treated more fully in this study, unfolding how our conscious being unites with the developing embryo, having had its own biography in the spiritual world between death and rebirth.

Highest of all is the incarnation of the Christ spirit into the earthly body of Jesus of Nazareth.

All levels of incarnation need preparation. At the smallest level, how we prepare for the night can affect how we wake in the morning. At the level of life and death, what we carry as karma from previous lives will have an effect on developmental processes as it interweaves with what is given by earthly heredity.

The incarnation of Christ needed a unique preparation. A spirit, stronger and purer than any of us, chose to come to the earth, not out of karmic necessity but out of love for humanity and compassion for its suffering. This spirit could not have entered directly into the ordinary embryological process, for its power would have been like a destroying fire. There was no 'Christ child' as is popularly thought. Instead, other real children had to be prepared so that Christ could incarnate into a human body. Who then was able to take on the body into which Christ was to incarnate, a body that would be able to resurrect? This also had to be carefully prepared. What was needed was a body of great purity, unimpaired by any karma, and also a consciousness that held all that could be learned on the earth. This needed two human beings, with different kinds of spiritual and earthly biographies. The Matthew and Luke Gospels tell the stories of these two individuals, both called Jesus. Their stories will unfold in this study.

The complex dynamic that accompanied the entry of the Christ spirit into earth existence is very different from the one that normally results in the birth of an ordinary human being. Nevertheless, Rudolf Steiner saw a connection between these two processes and called them both conceptions. He was the first to ever do this, and this study hopes to shed some light on this, beginning with the essential biological components of conception, ovum and sperm cells and the process by which they come into being as a polarity.

It is important to understand that the spiritual is not being diminished by being placed alongside the biological. The biological or organic has an essential spiritual component, and the spiritual has an essential earthly component. Both are expressions of a reality that is a fundamental gesture of the cosmos that embraces heaven and earth.

Biological Conception

Biological conception, or fertilisation, is a process familiar to most people, at least in its broad outline, and is central to everything that happens on the earth. Sexuality, the coming together of male and female, is the intense dynamic that serves this necessity of bringing sentient beings into existence, be that earthworms or lizards, lions or human beings. Only the most primitive of creatures have forms of asexual reproduction (not requiring a male/female polarity) – they have not reached the stage of evolution where oneness is separated into two and needs sexuality to bring about unity. All human beings are born of this unity, which is also the basis of an intense relationship between people.

The polarity of male and female is shown most clearly in the development and final form of the germ cells: the ovum and the sperm cell. This is not the same polarity as man and woman, however. Each human being incarnates into either a male or female body, but in the life of any particular human being, maleness and femaleness are interwoven in very individual and complex ways. Even the

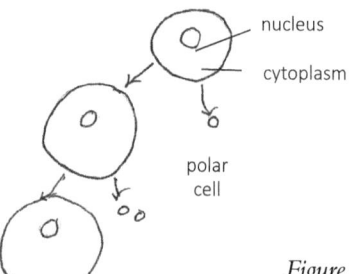

Figure 1. The immature germ cell

outer bodily characteristics are variable. In the germ cells, however, maleness and femaleness show themselves clearly and unequivocally and any deviation from this polarity is not viable. There is no diversity at the level of the cell.

The central purpose of germ cell development is to establish two kinds of cells that are polar to each other in almost all their characteristics (Figure 1). Both arise from simple cells that are indistinguishable from each other as far as gender is concerned. Both have the physical appearance (phenotype) of an archetypal cell, that is, with a cell membrane enclosing cytoplasmic substance and a nucleus with its own membrane having the DNA-bearing chromosomes within. This immature cell is round in form. Only the DNA (genotype) is different, the future ovum having two X chromosomes and the future sperm having an X and a Y chromosome.

The germ cells arise in a way that is unique in

embryological development. Nearly all cells will develop in the place where the future organ will be; for instance, liver cells develop where the liver will be. The germ cells are an exception to this. They arise in the two- to three-week old embryo, so that the next generation is already being prepared when the 'parent' is barely 1 mm in size. Around this time the embryo develops into three layers: the upper (ectoderm), the lower (endoderm) and between them the mesoderm. At about two weeks some cells break away from the upper layer and they migrate outside the embryo to what is called the yolk sack (remnant of the ovum cytoplasm). There they increase in number and then, at about the fourth week, they migrate back and take their place in the developing sexual organ, the ovary or the testis. They are like 'guests' in these organs for they belong to the next generation within a body that is yet to be born. It is only when they become part of the host-parent organ that they begin to differentiate into egg or sperm. Every stage of this development increases the polarity between them, a polarity that is not to be seen in the immature cells, which look exactly like each other.

Germ cell development

The male cell develops towards the centre of its host organ, the testis. During this journey each cell undergoes two rounds of specialised cell division known as meiosis.

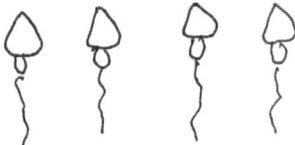

Figure 2. Mature sperm cells

This results in four 'daughter' cells, each having half the number of chromosomes, so that at conception and the fusion of cells the total number of chromosomes is restored. (The simpler, mitotic division of all other body cells produces two daughter cells each containing the same number of chromosomes as the parent cell.) During this process the male cells undergo an extreme extraction of the cytoplasmic component of the cell so that on maturity it consists predominately of nucleus. There is also an energy-generating middle section and a long motile tail. Thus, it is threefold: a script-bearing head, a force-bearing middle and a long motile tail (Figure 2). This familiar sperm form comes to maturity only at puberty, and from then onwards they are constantly created until the end of life. They are one of the most formed cells of the body and are viable only if fertilisation occurs, for they lack the necessary nutritional component which only the ovum can contribute. The sperm cells are all 'head' and lack almost everything else.

The ovum does the exact opposite in its development. In the two meiotic divisions that are needed to produce half the

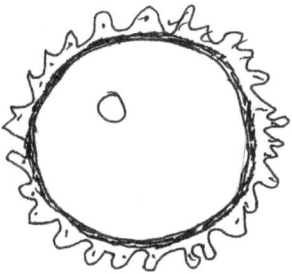

Figure 3. Mature ovum

number of chromosomes in each of the resulting daughter cells, the division is unequal, creating a single very large cell, the future ovum, and three very small cells that have no further known function. The ovum is predominately cytoplasm – the opposite of the sperm – and while it does of course retain a nucleus, it is the balance that is different (Figure 3). The ovum develops to maturity at the rate of one every month after puberty until the menopause. The maturation of each ovum takes place towards the periphery of the ovary, again polar to the sperm which matures towards the centre of its host organ, the testis.

Neither cell is viable without fertilisation. They are polar to each other but belong together in creating the wholeness of a new organism. The ovum is large, just about visible to the eye without a microscope and it is round in form. The sperm cell is tiny and very formed. Until recently this polarity has been seen as complete in every aspect of form and function. However, recent research has indicated that the ovum is not entirely passive, as it was thought, but seems to be able to 'choose' a sperm cell. At the moment, this 'choice' is understood to be based on both genetic and biochemical factors. The ovum seems to show a different kind of activity to that of the motile sperm, one that appears to be more sensitive and discerning.

To sum up, of the two cells that meet, 'maleness' is characterised by an intense activity driven by its own script-bearing form – the sperm cell. 'Femaleness' on the other hand is a much quieter but discerning substance-bearing form – the ovum, which after conception becomes the new human body.

Conception

The sperm cell and the ovum meet at conception, and as in all situations where tension is brought about by a polarity, a shock is created when that tension is suddenly released. Rudolf Steiner called it a chaos, rather than a shock. Biologically, it shows itself through the sperm immediately losing its form, the two sets of chromosomes – the male and female – are 'shaken up', some even breaking and joining up again in new combinations, and the cytoplasm of the cell is brought into a near chaotic state. Some researchers have seen the ovum light up at the moment of conception,

Figure 4. Fertilisation

and a structured wave visible with the microscope, passes round the outside of the cell (Figure 4). All of this breaks the cell free of the constraints of biological order, normally a necessity for all cell functions. It is a unique moment in the life of the organism.

The third element

Genetics alone cannot bring about the development of the human being. The genetic element of the cell carries a great amount of information in the form of a biochemical substance, but the human form itself, which is of a higher order, can only be found in the spiritual world. Rudolf Steiner called this the spirit germ, the spiritual forces of the physical body, and this can only enter into earthly conditions if the biological order is broken up, as happens at conception.

The spirit germ comes from the world we live in after death, and its creation is the essence of every human life, but we ourselves are not aware that during earthly life we bear a form that has its origin in the highest heavens.

When a human being dies, the spirit and soul leave the body immediately, while the life forces withdraw over a period of about three days. However, the spiritual form of the body remains with the physical substances after death. A new spirit germ therefore has to be created for the next life, and the subsequent journey of the soul and spirit through the spiritual world can be seen in this light. It can be called a journey because there is a destination, the highest realm that the soul can reach, furthest from the earthly sphere: the Midnight Hour of existence. Reaching it means crossing several thresholds, not only the one that is experienced here as death, but also the one where the etheric or life body is laid aside and we step into the soul world. Here the soul is purified, for only what is pure can enter the true spiritual world. What remains unpurified is unable to enter this highest world and is left behind and guarded so that it can be woven into the next earthly life as part of our karma. The spirit germ is woven at the Midnight Hour, when the 'I' has expanded until it is able to encompass the entire cosmos. Here on earth, we experience ourselves as having a centre which we call 'I'. There, at the Midnight

BIOLOGICAL CONCEPTION

Hour, we are pure spirit 'centred' in the periphery, that is, in the starry world of the zodiac. Out of that communion of centre and periphery the germ of a new body is created.

It is the most glorious of all the work that can be done, in heaven or here on earth. Here we see the body only from the outside, no matter how finely it may be dissected. From the spiritual inner aspect it is quite different. Rudolf Steiner has this to say about it:

> At a certain stage [of life after death, man] works with the spirits of the cosmos on ... the inner wisdom-filled structure of a physical human body by preforming it as a universal spirit germ ... But everything that happens in celestial existence is concealed in immeasurable depths in the physical organism in which man is clothed on earth ...
>
> This is the tragedy of materialism that it believes it can know matter, and speaks always of matter and its laws ... What materialism knows the least about is the material human organism. Not until materialism came into being did the complicated material structures of physical earth existence become as concealed as they now are from the otherwise admirable natural science of the present time.[2]

From the spiritual inside, our bodies are more beautiful and complex than any cathedral and this is our creative work when we reach the Midnight Hour. When the time comes to begin the journey towards a new incarnation, we are as unwilling to leave that place as we are to leave the earth at death.

On earth, the body and the 'I' dwelling in that body are not in the same kind of communion with each other as they are in the Midnight Hour. If they were we would be able to have full conscious control of all the processes of the body, such as the complex biochemical processes that take place in the liver and all the other organs. We do not have this and instead depend on a co-working of genetics, spiritual beings and the body-based representative of the individual spirit, sometimes called the ego organisation in anthroposophy.

The biological polarity of male/female is the representative of a higher principle that exists everywhere in the world of spirit. As one example, it appears as the polarity of life and form, the germ cells being a special case of this – the ovum is life, the sperm is form. In embryology, the growth of cells and the shaping of those cells to become an organ sometimes means the death of cells. An example of this is the formation of the hand, which begins as a paddle shape very early in development. The fingers are formed, not by outgrowths from this paddle, but through cells dying away between them to create the five digits. Life and death are both needed, and the balance between the two is what creates and sustains our health, even at the cellular level.

However, at the Midnight Hour of existence, at the furthest point from the earth, there is complete communion between those greatest of polarities, the centre as 'I' and the periphery where the form of the body is spread out across the zodiac. On the earth this 'I' is the gateway that leads from earthly experience to higher spiritual realities. And the highest of those realities is the creation of the spirit germ at the Midnight Hour. Our central spiritual being is able to create this out of the communion of centre and periphery. The intention of the spiritual world is that this communion shall also exist on the earth. It has happened only once in all of earth existence, and that was with the Resurrection Body of Christ. He was sent to fulfil this intention, so that each one of us will, in time, be able to reach that point.

In the very far past the human being was not divided into male and female. Both aspects were within one being and were capable of self-fructification. This was at the time when the earth was not as hard as it is now and so it was still possible for an incarnating human being to draw what was needed as substance out of the earth to create a new body. As the earth became denser this kind of metabolism was no longer possible, so the two aspects of the whole became slowly separated into outwardly distinguishable male and female. This needed the principles of heredity – genetics – to create a new human being in the place of self-fructification. (Some lower species of animal can still reproduce in this way.) So we became twofold, not only male or female, but also in the sense that for each human being, part of us is given through heredity and what flows through the generations, and part comes out of what the spirit has experienced on its journey through the Midnight Hour from the previous life.

In our present time the 'two becoming one' can only occur at the level of the cell at conception, which is well below our consciousness. We will look at how the 'two becoming one' occurred as a historical event on a level approaching our human consciousness later. But before looking at this, it is necessary to continue with the early stages of biological development.

Further development of the embryo

The fertilised ovum, now called the zygote, has a strong membrane around it called the zona pellucida. For as long as the membrane is there (which is about four days) the zygote has a stability that has a certain mineral quality. It can be frozen and then used in IVF treatment because the

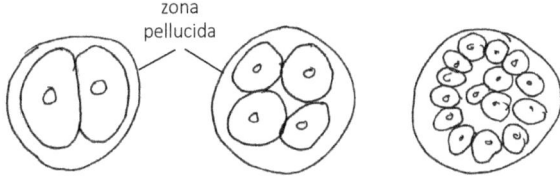

Figure 5. Cell divison from zygote to morula

membrane keeps it safe. Within the membrane the cells divide, although there is no visible differentiation between them at this point. The zygote is now called the morula (Figure 5). When the membrane dissolves allowing fluid to enter the morula, the first differentiation becomes visible. The cells at the periphery are destined to become the embryonic sheaths – amnion, allantois, and the chorion/placenta. The inner cell mass will become the embryo that, in time, will be born.

What happens first is the development of the sheaths, creating a 'house' in which the embryo is nourished, can grow and develop. Above the embryo the fluid-filled amnion develops (see Figure 6, overleaf). This will later surround it entirely when the embryonic disk folds into the recognisable human form. Underneath the embryonic disk is the yolk sack. When the folding takes place the yolk sack is drawn into the embryo to become the intestinal tract (see Figure 7). Surrounding it all is the chorion, which later becomes the placenta. During the nine months of

THE INCARNATION OF CHRIST: A SPIRITUAL EMBRYOLOGY

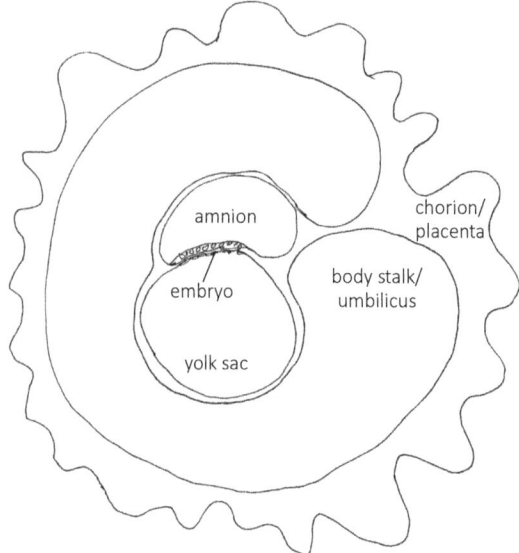

Figure 6. The embryo after 14 days

pregnancy it provides nutrition and facilitates excretion and breathing. It also allows the spirit to enter. In the womb the whole human being is body and sheaths. From the moment when these sheaths begin to form, growth cannot be stopped, the organism no longer has mineral qualities and so can no longer be preserved.

Once this growth has begun, the etheric is at work and the embryo must grow and metamorphose into human form. Metamorphosis, or differentiation, is like a reduction of possibilities. The morula, the original ball of cells, is multi-

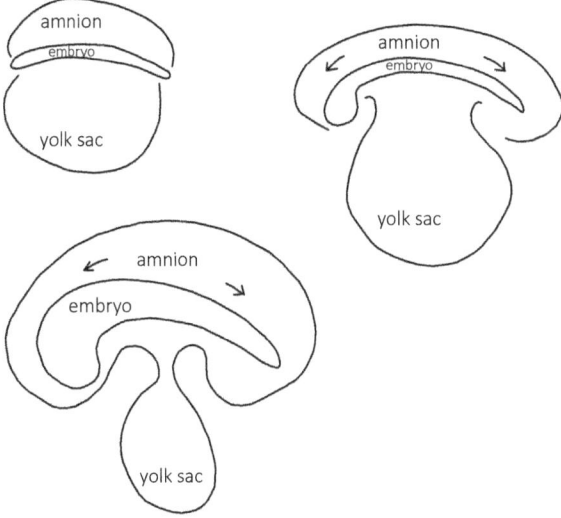

Figure 7. Folding of the embryo

potential – every cell could become a whole organism. It is all there but in seed form. Differentiation means that choices have been made, and cells now form part of an arm or the brain or the liver; multi-potentiality is lost and the form emerges. This is one of the mysteries of embryology, from the formless 'all' to the visible but limited part.

At this stage the incarnating soul and spirit are still abiding in the spiritual world, but near to the earth. Only the spirit germ has incarnated into substance at conception and is therefore also present with the forces of heredity in sperm and ovum. The two fundamental parts of us – the form (spirit germ) and the spirit that belongs to it (the 'I') – have been separated from each other in our pre-birth existence between Midnight Hour and conception, because the spirit germ belongs to the earthly human form and the 'I' belongs to the heavens. At the Midnight Hour they were united and fundamentally belong to each other, so that a kind of longing for the lost communion draws the 'I' nearer, wishing to unite with what is already on the earth.

However, in order to do this, etheric forces have to be drawn out of the cosmos that will unite the spiritual with what is already the earthly. Not just any etheric forces, but the ones that include the unresolved karma from the previous incarnation. Rudolf Steiner speaks quite humorously of this, describing how this karma has been kept in a kind of left luggage office until it is claimed and delivered into the etheric forces of the incarnating soul.[3] It is at this time, at about seventeen days, that the invisible human (the 'I') can come nearer.

The sheaths have already built the 'house' for the human being to inhabit – a house with several rooms. There is a fluid room, the amnion, in which the child floats until birth. There is an airy, warmth room, the chorion/placenta, from which the soul-spiritual forces unfold and have their influence, as well as all the physiological factors that are needed. The individual spirit enters the placenta at about seventeen or eighteen days after conception. At this point the higher spirit, the 'I', comes near to the embryo, but only as far as the chorion/placenta. It does not enter directly into the embryo. If this were to happen, the absolute truth that our higher 'I' bears would be too difficult for us to endure during our earthly life. It would leave us unfree, unable to make mistakes and thereby learn from them. So the higher spirit works from the placenta and only to the extent that it is karmically right for any incarnating soul. The hereditary forces and the spirit germ working together can do a great deal within the developing embryo. However, the time in the womb is the closest that our higher being comes to us and it influences development in very individual ways.

The importance of the placenta is something that many ancient civilisations were aware of. For instance, in ancient Egypt when the Pharaoh went among his people in procession an image of his placenta was carried in front of him, as the bearer of his true higher spirit that could directly connect to the gods.

Birth is separation from the sheaths and what they carry. The placenta is discarded. Throughout pregnancy it has provided the embryo with nutrition and managed breathing, excretion and many other physiological factors as well as higher individual guidance. Only that spiritual part does not enter fully into the body, giving it instead an image of itself, called the ego-organisation, which humanises the biological and the genetic. The higher spirit excarnates at birth as the placenta dies. Our earthly spirit, the one we call 'I' throughout our life, retains a connection to its higher being and can bring it consciously into gradual incarnation.

To sum up, human incarnation is a twofold process. The form of the body incarnates first, immediately at conception, and permeates both the future body and its sheaths. Next, the 'I' incarnates usually around the eighteenth day into the prepared chorion (later the placenta), and from there it then works on the future body.

Christological Embryology

It is at this point where ordinary embryology has brought us to the threshold of an awareness of the higher 'I', that we can begin to consider a Christological embryology as Rudolf Steiner spoke of it in *The Fifth Gospel*. In what ways can it be compared to the ordinary embryology and in what ways is it different? At the biological level, conception is the only situation where two cells become one, and it is something that takes place well below our consciousness. One cell then divides into two, and it continues this way until there are trillions of cells that differentiate into the human body. Can this same gesture – two becoming one and the creation of a body – be found at a higher level? Has there been in the history of humanity a situation where two becoming one has happened at a level closer to, or even above, our human consciousness rather than below it?

To begin with, let us return to the passage from *The Fifth Gospel,* quoted in the Introduction, in which Steiner compares the Baptism in the Jordan to something like human conception when the Christ spirit entered Jesus of

Nazareth. This moment can be seen as having the same quality as the meeting of the spirit germ with the fertilised ovum at conception. Both forms of conception result in a body: in the ordinary, biological sense, a human body, in the higher Christological one, the Resurrection Body.

But what about the processes that precede the spirit germ uniting with the fertilised ovum? Is there anything in this view of a Christological conception that can be compared to them? According to Steiner they are reflected in two events that precede the Baptism.

The first is the birth of Jesus as described by Matthew and Luke. In *The Fifth Gospel* Rudolf Steiner makes it clear that there were in fact two Jesus children, born to two different families, and that the birth of these two boys was a human incarnation – each with a father and mother, and each with a human 'I' as a spirit germ.

The second event was the union of these two Jesus children in which the spirit of the one united with the body of the other. This is alluded to in the Gospel of Luke in the story of the twelve-year-old Jesus in the temple. In this event there are male and female elements that come together, but unlike in human conception, the higher spirit, the 'I', does not enter after eighteen days, but only after eighteen years when the Christ spirit enters the body of Jesus of Nazareth. Here, too, is a kind of foreshadowing of the higher conception and birth, which is the 'conception' at the Baptism and the 'birth' at the death and resurrection on Golgotha.

The birth in the Gospel of Matthew

All four gospels begin with birth stories, but only Matthew and Luke with the birth of Jesus. Mark begins with the Baptism in the Jordan, the beginning of Christ's existence on earth. The Gospel of John begins with the eternal birth of the Word, existing from the beginning of all things, and now becoming flesh in Jesus Christ.

The gospels that begin with the birth of Jesus are very different from each other in almost every way. Matthew's Gospel tells the story of a boy born of a long ancestry that begins with Abraham, an individual who lived within the time frame of human history. One could say that Abraham was the father of the events of the Old Testament. The genealogy at the beginning of the gospel follows the paternal line from Abraham to King David and then continues through David's son King Solomon down to Joseph, the father of Jesus. This Jesus, then, is born of the kingly line of Solomon, who was renowned for his wisdom and discernment. He built the first temple as a permanent home for the tablets given to Moses on Mount Sinai that contained the laws by which the Hebrew people lived.

Until Solomon built the temple, they had journeyed across the desert from place to place until they came to Canaan, which had been given to them as their Holy Land.

In Matthew's Gospel the Annunciation telling of the birth of Jesus is given to Joseph of the Solomon line. The predominant image of the Annunciation, the one we are most familiar with, comes from Luke's Gospel in which the archangel Gabriel appears to Mary. It is difficult to find a painting of the Annunciation to Joseph; they do exist, but they do not have the memorable quality of the paintings of the Annunciation to Mary. The message about the birth of Jesus is told to Joseph in a dream after he learns that his betrothed, Mary, is with child and he quietly decides to divorce her. Only then does the angel speak to him in a dream, telling him of the nature of the child that will be born: 'Do not be afraid to take Mary home as your wife, because what is conceived in her is from the Holy Spirit' (Mt 1:19–20).

This presents us immediately with a riddle. If Joseph is the earthly father of the child born of the kingly Solomon line, what then does it mean if the Holy Spirit is also described as the father? Here, a return to embryology is helpful. Every child is born out of a hereditary stream and also out of the spirit: the spirit germ and the higher 'I' come from heaven and work together with an earthly substance that is permeated by the forces of heredity. So also with Jesus, but with a spirit greater than the individual. This is the Spirit that embraces all of humanity, the Holy Spirit. Joseph was indeed the father – Rudolf Steiner describes how conception took place whilst both Joseph and Mary were in a kind of sleep – so both the biological and spiritual aspects of conception were truly unconscious.

All the heavenly messages in the Matthew birth story are given to Joseph while dreaming. The instructions from the angel to take mother and child to safety in Egypt and to return again when the vicious King Herod has died, are all given in sleep. The three kings themselves are informed in a dream not to return to Herod, who is awaiting confirmation of the birth of the Messiah, and so journey home by another way. Only Herod does not dream; he is unable to receive spiritual substance about the future at that depth. Instead, he refers back to the already ossified law to discover where the Messiah is to be born, and, furious at not seeing the three kings again, orders all boys in Bethlehem and its vicinity who are two years old or younger to be killed in the hope that he will catch Jesus among them. In this gospel the preparation for the incarnation of Christ is full of danger. We hear almost nothing of Mary or of the child, except that after returning from Egypt they settle in Nazareth. The story then continues with the Baptism in the Jordan.

Matthew's story is full of activity. There are journeys – of the family to Egypt and back, of the kings to Herod and the child and then back to their own lands. All are full of intention and divinely ordained. There is the terrible activity of Herod and the killing of the children. In this gospel there is very little stillness, apart from the holy family itself and the worship of the kings as they give their gifts. Much else is concerned with the flight from evil and the struggle to realise the divine on the earth. Alongside all of this there is wisdom. There is the star knowledge of the kings that lead them to the child and there is the wisdom that must have surrounded the family during their years in Egypt. There is even the knowledge that lay in the law that told of 'a ruler who will shepherd my people Israel' (Mt 2:6). The Matthew story is wisdom and will, as well as evil and danger.

One element stands out, however: the messages to both Joseph and the kings from the spiritual world are always given in dreams. Their daytime consciousness is not able to receive the words of the angel directly. It may seem paradoxical that the male element in this birth story is associated with dream consciousness. Rudolf Steiner says about this in *Cosmic Memory* that the division of the sexes into male and female led eventually to a certain situation:

> The force by which mankind forms a thinking brain for itself is the same by which man impregnated himself in ancient times. The price of thought is single sexedness.[4]

And again:

> The average brain of a man has overstepped a certain general point of evolution; it has become drier, more wooden ... The male brain is stiff, resistant, and more difficult to manipulate than a female brain ... Consequently, the female brain can more quickly follow what is new in our view of the world.[5]

Although Rudolf Steiner is describing this evolutionary process in general and certainly not in direct relation to the gospels, it is easy to imagine that even in those times, someone like Joseph had a less imaginative consciousness of the world, meaning the spirit could enter only in dreams. When he awoke, he did not question what he had been told but did immediately what the angel said. The male element is emphasised in Matthew's Gospel; the softer female side is barely there.

The birth in the Gospel of Luke

Luke's Gospel begins with yet another conception and incarnation, that of John the Baptist, a figure central to the story of Christ. His father, Zachariah, was a priest of the temple in Jerusalem. One day, as he is burning incense at the altar, he is visited by the archangel Gabriel who tells him that his wife will bear a son. Zachariah questions this, for his wife, Elizabeth, is already too old to bear children. This is a very modern response and one that would be used to this day, but Zachariah is told in no uncertain terms not to question the word of God who makes all things possible. He becomes mute and remains so until John is born. From the perspective of this study the story lies between Matthew and Luke. Zacariah was awake when he received the message – no doubt in a raised consciousness being near the altar – but still he could not accept it because of his way of thinking. He is given time to learn.

Intertwined with the birth story of John is that of Mary and the birth of Jesus. The whole focus is on Mary, we hear little of Joseph. She, too, is visited by the archangel Gabriel, and she is awake when she is told of the birth and the destiny of the child that she will bear. She also questions this, 'How shall this be since I have no husband?' This is subtly different from Zachariah's question, 'How shall I know this?' Knowing and being relate to different aspects of the human soul. Mary is not scolded for her question but is simply told the process by which she will conceive and bear a child. 'The Holy Spirit will come upon you, and the power of the Most High will overshadow you' (Lk 1:35). Her own consciousness will become a servant or handmaiden to the higher spirit of all humanity. Zachariah is given the chance to grow and learn; Mary, with her already open and receptive consciousness, is told what will befall her. This is different only in magnitude from the conception of every human being. In every conception there is an opening for the incarnation of the individuality, but in Mary, that was the individuality for the salvation of humanity.

The message of Gabriel to Mary also carried another element that was essential for Mary to know: the importance of the relationship of the newly conceived Jesus with the being of John, already six months in the womb of Elizabeth, wife of Zachariah. The two women meet, bringing about the first encounter between the two children. Through the presence of Mary and the child she carried, Elizabeth felt the first movements of the unborn John. They remained together for some time, allowing the two unborn ones to live in that relationship, something so profound that it would later lead Jesus to

John to be baptised. Their meeting was ordained by the angelic world before their earthly life.

The stories of the two women are clothed in words of glory, expressed in the Magnificat (Lk 1:46–55) which has a fulness of heart knowledge. Elizabeth has words of revelation and joy, all brought forth by the meeting of the two of them and of their children. This is the feminine element: almost overwhelmed by the greatness of an event, the women give their words divine devotional and poetic content.

The birth of Jesus in Luke's Gospel is embedded in nature, taking place in a stable in the presence of animals. In Matthew's Gospel, the birth of the Matthew child is embedded in the stars, as well as in the knowledge of scripture used by Herod as his support. The shepherds in Luke are also embedded in nature. Shepherds in that part of the world were not the quaint figures that we might associate with the traditional plays like the Oberufer Shepherds' Play, they were strong and awake human beings. The shepherds in the gospel learn about the birth of Jesus in a revelation from the heavens, not in the language of the stars, or even a guiding star, but directly from the angel as Mary did. They are not dreaming. They go and 'see' what had been revealed to them spiritually. This is a very different kind of perception from the dreams of Matthew's Gospel.

Luke's Gospel also has a genealogy, but it comes at the end of the birth story and after the Baptism in the Jordan, after thirty years had passed. In that sense the emphasis is on the Christ in Jesus Christ, while Matthew places the emphasis on the Jesus in Jesus Christ. The Luke genealogy is different from Matthew's. It begins with Jesus, the son of Joseph, and works backwards in time through his ancestors to Nathan, the son of King David. Then there are the many generations back to Abraham, which agree with those of the Matthew genealogy that goes in the opposite direction. Then Luke continues back from Abraham to Adam, the Son of God. Matthew's genealogy goes forward in the direction of the wisdom gathered on earth, while Luke's goes backwards along the path of wisdom that proceeds directly from God.

When we compare the two stories, we can see two different gestures. Luke is full of a cosmic expansion that allows heaven and earth to meet in creative relationship. In this study this is called 'female'. The gesture of Matthew's Gospel is much more that of contraction. The kings show this in the power of concentration and thinking needed to understand what the star they are following is saying to them, even if the result of this effort is as wide as the heavens themselves. There is a difference between this and the power of revelation with which the Luke story is steeped, contraction showing itself in the difficulty in finding a place for the child to be born. The two, expansion and contraction, always go together, only the emphasis is different in each gospel. The Gospel of Matthew, with its danger and pain and Herod's deceit, emphasises contraction. This gesture is called 'male' in this study. The two gospels show a polarity, and like all polarities they belong together. How is this to happen if we are speaking about people and not cells? The mastery of polarities is a matter that has accompanied human beings from the beginning until the present day. To find some answers to this question requires looking at a deeper picture.

The spiritual background to the Matthew story

In order to deepen the pictures given in the gospel, it is necessary to look at the spiritual background given by Rudolf Steiner in two of his lecture cycles, *The Fifth Gospel* and *According to Matthew*. From these sources it becomes clear that one has to go much further back in time than Matthew's genealogy, which begins with Abraham. We have to go back to the fall of Atlantis, described in Genesis as the Great Flood, when streams of people migrated eastwards into Europe and Asia.

From there, one stream went south into what is now India. The people who settled there developed the ability to look into the spirit as it had been at its highest point in Atlantis, and they regarded the surrounding sense world as fallen and illusory (maya). Another stream went north into what is now Russia and Siberia. They lived out of a lower kind of vision, a ritual shamanism that gave them some power over nature. They were nomads and exploiters of nature, not protectors of it. And a third stream remained in the area now called Iran. They were also aware that the purest spiritual vision of Atlantis was no longer available to them, but they saw that the sense world had fallen as much as human beings had fallen. Instead of denying it, or using it, they saw that it needed to be led upwards again, towards the spirit, to a new point in evolution that worked in a balanced way with the external world. Out of this group emerged a great spiritual leader, Zarathustra. Through his inspired teaching and his leadership in working with nature, farming – the development of agriculture and animal husbandry – began.

This cannot be done through a dream consciousness. It can only be done through thinking. So Zarathustra was the first to develop the thinking that was needed to master and care for nature. His spiritual teaching led to outer activity, wakefulness and the conviction that human beings could be led forward with nature to reach the highest spirit (whom he called Ahura Mazdao), rather than back to what had been great in the past. He sought a balance between heaven and earth – the spirit and the sense world. In this way he was a pre-Christian Christian. Rudolf Steiner described how the individuality of Zarathustra appeared again in outer human civilisation in the sixth century BC as Nazarathos, or Zarathos. In this incarnation he became the teacher of the wisest Hebrew pupils who were being held in captivity in Babylon. During this period, the Hebrews developed what is now recognised as Judaism, with its extreme separateness that was needed to preserve their identity in a foreign culture, and to hold them to the worship of Yahweh. Around this time Zarathustra was also the teacher of Pythagoras.

What concerns us here, however, is the subsequent incarnation of this individuality as the Jesus of the Solomon line described in Matthew's Gospel. This boy had not only a kingly heredity, but his spiritual past was as one of the oldest and wisest individualities of humanity, having gathered a vast store of initiation wisdom over the course of many incarnations. We all have this double origin: an inherited one and a spiritual one. In the Jesus boy of Matthew's Gospel, both were of the highest.

The spiritual background to the Luke story

The genealogy of the Gospel of Luke leads back to Adam and then to God. In a way, that could be said about every human being – do we not all go back to God? For most of us that would be hard to trace, but in Luke's Gospel it is very specific because all the ancestors are named, right back to God. It is as if the hereditary stream and the spiritual stream are one. Rudolf Steiner spoke of this in his cycle of lectures about this gospel (*According to Luke*). The genealogies of the two gospels are the same between Abraham and David, then they part. Matthew's Gospel follows the kingly line through David and his son Solomon, and from there to Joseph, the father of Jesus. But David had another son, Nathan. Who was he? Very little is said about him in the Bible. He is mentioned only three times, but not with any great emphasis. He was the father of two sons who may have been priests, and he is mentioned in the Book of Zechariah as part of a prophecy. In Luke's Gospel, his descendant was Joseph, the father of Jesus.

In this study, this child is referred to as the Nathan or Luke Jesus, the Matthew child is the Solomon or Matthew Jesus.

However, there is a question that can be asked about the Nathan lineage that goes back to Adam. When Adam and Eve were expelled from paradise, did it remain empty? Rudolf Steiner tells us something about this in *According to Luke*:

> A certain portion of the ether body's forces were retained ... Some of Adam's forces were taken from him after the Fall, and this innocent part of Adam was preserved in the great mother lodge of humanity ... This aspect of Adam's soul had not been involved in events leading up to the Fall and was therefore untouched by human guilt.[6]

In the work of Rudolf Steiner, this soul is always referred to as the Nathan soul. Who was that soul before he incarnated into the Luke child? We need to imagine that in the far past when the being of Adam was not yet a clearly defined image that we would recognise as a human being, part of Adam remained there, in the garden of Eden, a part sometimes called his 'sister-soul'. This being was filled with human potential, but did not go through the Fall as Adam did.

Much happened to this pure human soul between these events at the beginning of creation and the time when he entered into the Jesus child of Luke's Gospel. This Nathan soul was not, to begin with, ready for an earthly incarnation, but had a form like a paradisal angel. In this form in which he lived in the spiritual world he could not have entered directly into a human form of hereditary origin. He had to be made ready for life on earth. In a single lecture, 'The Pre-

Earthly Deeds of Christ', Rudolf Steiner describes what this preparation involved. Three events occurred that were all spiritual precursors of the Mystery of Golgotha, except they did not take place on earth. Only the fourth event, the Mystery of Golgotha itself, occurred in the sense world. These events were as important for the evolution of every human being on the earth as the Mystery of Golgotha.

The angelic form of the Nathan soul would not have been suitable for the future incarnation of Christ on earth. But for that incarnation to be possible, a human being needed to be born who possessed all the possibilities of the guiltless pre-Fall human soul – the Nathan soul. Christ therefore had to bring about certain developments in this soul so that, in time, he himself could incarnate on earth in the purest possible body. The angelic Nathan form had to become 'fit' for the earth. All three of these events were alike to the Mystery of Golgotha in that Christ incarnated in the Nathan being who was still in the spiritual world. All three effected changes in the Nathan being that brought him nearer to what would be needed on the earth when Christ incarnated there.

The first of these occurred during Lemuria, and enabled evolving human beings to raise themselves from the horizontal and stand upright. Through the earthly forces of heredity this allowed the evolving human form to develop muscle-bone coordination and balance, so that only the soles of our feet need to touch the earth and bear our weight. We see this reflected in the development of every child who learns first to crawl and then to stand upright. Every child learning to walk upright is a recapitulation of this period in Lemuria. The earth itself has nothing to offer human beings by way of an impulse to stand upright. Nathan was the angel-like being with human ancestry (Adam) who could bring about something new on the earth. Without this pre-earthly deed of Christ, this first stage of Golgotha, the powers of nature would have prevailed and human beings would have remained horizontal, like the animals. The other side of this deed is that the Nathan being, now having a human form (though not a human body), surrendered his angelic form in order to find his place on the earth.

The second event occurred during Atlantis. Once again, the Nathan being, now possessing a human form, allowed himself to be permeated by Christ. Through this, the organs of speech and breathing were fashioned so that human beings could make sounds that were not merely expressions of their own sensations and emotions, but which related to the world around them. It is inherent in every child to move from entirely subjective sound, by imitation to words that can describe the world. That was the second pre-earthly deed in Christ's preparation for his descent.

There was a third event, later in the Atlantean period, which led to the development of language and thus the ability to think. With this came the subsequent emerging, or incarnation, of the 'I'. Again, the pure Nathan being offered himself to Christ, bringing about the third pre-earthly deed of Christ, the third stage of the Mystery of Golgotha.

All of these stages took place in the worlds of spirit and can be seen as events in the journey of Christ to the earth. In Steiner's lecture, the fourth stage, which took place on the earth, is described in this way:

> The fourth Christ-event, the Mystery of Golgotha, took place so that ... thinking might also be connected to the Christ impulse, and not lapse into disorder in its effect on the 'I'.[7]

We usually think of Christ as overcoming death rather than being involved with the other pole of existence, that of birth and growth. The earthly stage of the Mystery of Golgotha did rescue humanity from death and overcame the densest state of spirit, which is matter. The unique greatness of this event cannot be overemphasised, which is why it is called the Turning Point of Time. However, when the angelic Nathan being was transformed through

Christ in the pre-earthly stages of Golgotha, this being developed the abilities of uprightness, speech and thought for all humanity. These faculties are linked to that part of Adam which did not go through the Fall – the Nathan being. Whereas the Adam who experienced the Fall and was expelled from the Garden of Eden began that line of evolution in which humanity has much in common with the rest of nature. It is the pre-Fall abilities of uprightness, speech and thought that makes us into human beings. They come directly from the spirit. Here we see Christ's participation in birth, growth, and ultimately in human embryology.

From this, it becomes clear that there are two streams of evolution in us: the pre-earthly Nathan stream and the earthly Adam stream. These two are deeply entwined with each other, and necessarily so. We can call the earthly Adam stream the Darwinian stream, and although it cannot evolve the principles that make us human, despite its mastery of nature, it can provide the bodily basis for what is spiritual in us. The participation of Christ in the upbuilding of human development as well as in the processes of death and resurrection, is a very important motif in any higher embryology for it tells us that the Gospel of Luke is the continuation of the Nathan biography that had its beginnings with God, as the genealogy makes clear.

★

To sum up this section: the two children, both called Jesus with parents called Mary and Joseph, show us a polarity that is here called male and female, not only in the gospel stories but in the spiritual background to these stories. The Zarathustra individuality incarnated in the Matthew boy, bringing with him all the knowledge, wisdom, teaching and leadership amassed during his many incarnations. The Nathan being, who had never been on the earth before, incarnated in the Luke child. He brought with him an open soul and an infinite capacity for self-sacrifice, allowing him to be permeated once again by Christ. It is what happens next that brings biological embryology and a higher Christological embryology close to each other.

The twelve-year-old in the temple

In the Gospel of Matthew, following the nativity, we hear of the holy family's flight into Egypt to escape from Herod and of their return once Herod has died. Both journeys are instigated by an angel appearing to Joseph in a dream. The holy family return, not to Judea but to the safety of Nazareth in Galilee. Then we hear nothing until the time of the Baptism in the Jordan.

It is the Gospel of Luke, the gospel of the Nathan Jesus, that records another event in detail (Lk 2). In this gospel, the family travel from Nazareth to Jerusalem for the annual Passover festival. The temple in Jerusalem was the only place of true ritual where offerings could be made – synagogues were places of teaching, not of religious action. One can imagine streams of people on the roads leading to the city. It was a pilgrimage but also a great social occasion with many families greeting each other, eating together and conversing. Taking the account of two Jesus boys into consideration, it is not difficult to imagine that the two boys knew each other, both coming from Nazareth, and even that there was a bond of friendship between them.

At the end of the festival, when the father of each family has made his offering and all have worshipped, they return home, taking plenty of time and allowing for more social interaction. A day passes before the parents notice that Jesus is not with them. They turn back towards Jerusalem to look for him. After three days they find him in the temple. In what follows, normal, everyday life is suffused by a unique mystery experience. Jesus is listening to the great teachers of the temple, asking them questions and answering theirs in turn. His parents, like everyone there, are astonished. Full of anxiety they scold the boy and ask the kind of question we would be familiar with today: 'Why have you treated us like this?' The answer they receive is not one they would have expected from such a simple but loving boy: 'Did you not know that I must be in my Father's house?' No longer the father, Joseph, but the Father of all things.

This is the outward story, but full of hints that there is something much deeper happening. It is a mystery event that has entered the sense world, witnessed by many in the temple. This is one of the very few places in the New Testament where someone's age is given; we are told that the boy was twelve. (Another occasion is in Luke 3:23 after the Baptism in the Jordan, when we are told that Jesus began his ministry at the age of thirty.)

One can imagine that this Nathan boy was not in the least bit clever in terms of earthly knowledge, for he had never incarnated before, but he had the wisdom of the heart. This paradisal being, who had offered himself three times to Christ in the spiritual world, bringing about uprightness, speech and thought in the development of humanity, did not possess the treasures of earthly experience that the Zarathustra soul did. Instead, he was endowed with treasures from heaven: a fathomless capacity for love and empathy, and perhaps something magical as well – in his presence people felt well. Then, suddenly, in the temple, he could think and discuss things that belonged to age-old spiritual traditions. Little wonder his parents and everyone present were shocked.

The spiritual background to the temple story

It is necessary to move away for a moment from the conundrum of the temple scene and look at what anthroposophy tells us about it. There must have been a strong bond between the two boys growing up in Nazareth, of the kind that children often develop and one in which they both intuitively understood the differences between them. The Zarathustra boy able to perceive and understand the stream of religious and cultural life to which they both belonged, and the Nathan boy able to immediately understand other people. Rudolf Steiner explained in *The Fifth Gospel* that this deep bond had a unique consequence. The Zarathustra boy was able to give his wisdom-filled spirit to the other child, who had only a provisional 'I' and not one that had experienced many incarnations.

In terms of the theme of this study, we could say that this provisional 'I' of the Luke child was 'fertilised' by the wisdom-bearing 'I' of the Matthew child. This is a mystery deed. It is like a foreshadowing of the greater event – the entry of Christ into Jesus at the Baptism in the Jordan. In this study, these events can be considered from an embryological standpoint. In biological fertilisation, the meeting of male and female cells brings about a disturbance in the cell, loosening its inherent order and allowing the third component to enter the cell – the new human being. This is the entry of the spirit germ, the spiritual forces of the physical body, the impulse that will be followed later by the incarnation of the higher 'I' into the placenta.

In the higher conception we are not studying cells but human beings, so we have to think of this in a different way. Is there a disturbance in the being of Jesus of Nazareth that allows for a new element to enter human evolution? The higher conception would seem to have two stages: the uniting of the Solomon 'I' (maleness) with the Nathan soul and body (femaleness), and the higher one of the incarnation or conception of Christ into Jesus at the Jordan. Between these two events there are eighteen years, and in *The Fifth Gospel* Steiner speaks of this period as one of great disturbance for the soul of Jesus.

Neither child would necessarily have sensed what happened to them in the temple. It was a mystery event guided by the spirit but having its consequences in consciousness. The spirit knew what needed to happen for the destiny of the earth to be fulfilled. From this moment onwards the Gospel of Luke is the story of a whole human being with a deep wisdom and a profoundly loving and open heart. It is important to realise that the body that goes forward to death and resurrection is that of the Nathan child, offered to Christ long before earth existence. Of course, there is the inherited element of that body, with a long, carefully prepared genealogy. Without that there could be no earthly substance, but this body was not disturbed by any karmic elements from earlier earth lives. The Luke Jesus was as near to a pure body as it is possible to be.

This Luke Jesus was twelve years old when the event in the temple took place. The Gospel is very specific about this. Why is it so important that we know this? What happens at this age? It is around this time that puberty begins, during which every human being experiences profound changes in both body and soul. Rudolf Steiner describes this in a very rich way, not specifically in relation to the gospel, but about every human being.[8]

According to Steiner, when a child is born it is only their physical body that becomes independent of the mother; in all other respects they are still dependent. At seven years old the child's etheric or life body slowly becomes independent from the mother in a highly differentiated process that sees the protective maternal etheric sheath slowly develop into the child's own etheric sheaths. This takes place between the ages of seven and fourteen and frees up the forces of the etheric body for, among other things, thinking.

This period also involves changes to the spiritual sheathes surrounding the heart. The heart does of course have an etheric sheath during the child's time in the womb and after the birth, but it is mostly given through heredity and is not yet individual. This changes during these years. The individual etheric heart begins to absorb an image of the sun, moon and stars to replace the inherited, mostly maternal heart. This means that at this early adolescent point in life the heart is at its most cosmic and sensitive. Great changes begin to take place and the individual soul or astral body becomes independent, meeting what comes to it from the cosmos. This 'new' heart begins to record everything that happens – every step, movement and action this person does. It is the beginning of individual karma, and it takes place in the heart.

Every human being undergoes this transformation. It is a time of tender openness, sensitivity and receptivity. It is the time when young people can have an individual awareness of Christ in their life, when the sacrament of Confirmation takes place. They cannot be much older than fourteen, for after that the cosmic images in the etheric heart begin to fade, not entirely, but enough to close down some of that openness. The adolescent is 'born' with all the difficulties this might bring. The awareness of the spirit, and the relationship to Christ, must then be cared for consciously for it is no longer a given. It is the beginning of conscience and personal responsibility.

The two boys are a very special example of this mystery, which happens in a small way for every human being. We all conceive a new heart at this age, bringing cosmic forces into earthly life. What happened in the temple was also a kind of conception as the wisdom bearing 'I' of the Zarathustra boy entered the provisional 'I' of the Nathan boy. The former gave his whole spiritual being to the latter who existed on earth for the first time: the two became one. The Luke child continued on, but the Matthew boy, without an 'I', died soon after, having completed his task for that incarnation. In biological conception, too, the male cell quickly disappears and could be said to die. The union of a pure body with a wisdom bearing 'I' is a fundamental step towards the Mystery of Golgotha. The relation between these two mighty events is stated clearly by Rudolf Steiner:

> Once again, as at puberty [when he was twelve], a new 'I' filled the inner being of the Nathanic Jesus, but this time on a more universally significant level.[9]

All of that is a description of a higher conception that takes place between the two Jesus boys, and it has its earthly reflection in physical conception. The fusion of the polarities of maleness (Matthew) and femaleness

The two Jesus boys in Ambrogio Borgognone's Jesus in the Temple, *Basilica di Sant'Ambrogio, Milan, Italy.*

(Luke) give rise to something that is completely new in consciousness. In biological conception, the moment of meeting has a fleeting, disabling effect on the fertilised ovum, meaning that the precision of the cell order is loosened, allowing the spirit germ to enter from another realm. In the higher conception this also happens, but in a different way, since we are concerned with human beings of enormous complexity, and not with relatively simple cells, complex as they are. The disorder or loosening of Jesus of Nazareth takes much longer and takes place in the soul. It takes eighteen years between the temple event and the Baptism in the Jordan, when something like a universal spirit germ, the Christ-being, enters into earth existence.

There is a shift in the balance between hereditary and spiritual forces. Biological conception emphasises the hereditary aspect and the forces that come from the past. The future for any human being, however, lies in the strength or weakness of the incarnating 'I' and how it is able to work from the placenta. With this higher conception, a unique event on the earth, occurring only once, the Christ-spirit entered earth existence. Here the emphasis is on the future spiritual forces of both the Solomon and Nathan children in their total cooperation with Christ. And Christ works only for the future. After the temple event, it is the Nathan Jesus, inspired by the wisdom of the Zarathustra spirit, who goes on to ultimately experience death and resurrection.

What remains unanswered is whether the hereditary forces given to Christ through both children and their long genealogies go through a transformation at the resurrection. Have they done their work and no longer have a role to play? And does matter, the most condensed form of spirit, play any part in the Resurrection?

The lost eighteen years

There is silence in the four gospels between the event in the temple and the Baptism in the Jordan, a silence of eighteen years. Only Rudolf Steiner in *The Fifth Gospel* gives an account of those years and their central importance in understanding the earthly biography of Jesus. Firstly, he describes the experiences of the young Nathan boy after he became permeated by the Zarathustra being and all the new possibilities this brought about. Nobody in his immediate family understood what was happening to him, and he himself was unaware that the spirit of his friend was now working in him. Steiner describes the boy's loneliness. He knew everything about human culture and thought and still possessed tremendous forces of empathy; he knew this experience was given to him for a reason, but he did not know what that reason was.

The meeting of the two forms of consciousness aroused existential questions in the young boy. Zarathustra's knowledge would be for Jesus a burning reality that needed answers. He began to search for the very centre of spiritual endeavour, which would nourish humanity in the future and which Zarathustra knew of as the working of Ahura Mazda, the sun spirit. Surely the sages of the temple in Jerusalem would know this. But the more Jesus sought this, the more he saw that the Judaic tradition in which he had been raised could not measure up to the spiritual realities that had enlightened the prophets. The voice of Yahweh that had inspired the prophets, known as the *Bat Kol* in Hebrew tradition, was now silent. The working of Zarathustra in the Nathan Jesus was an inspiration and an intuition of what the future had to bring, but he could find no basis for this in the Judaic culture that surrounded him. One can only imagine the inner disturbance this brought about.

Then, in his trade as a carpenter, Jesus travelled widely. There are many legends about the journeys he is supposed to have taken during this time, not least the one in which he comes to Britain. We need only think of the poem 'Jerusalem' by William Blake, so central to the English folk soul: 'And did those feet in ancient time, / Walk upon England's mountains green.' Between the ages of eighteen and twenty-four, Jesus of Nazareth visited the places of the old pagan mysteries. But they too had declined, becoming not just weaker but depraved. Their temples were pervaded by demons and evil spirits that brought disease and spiritual collapse to the local populations. It was in one such place that the congregation, longing for redemption and renewal, tried to make him their priest. But as they lifted him up to their altar, Jesus of Nazareth fell down as though dead. In a state of altered consciousness, he heard the voice of the *Bat Kol,* now transformed, speak a macrocosmic prayer that described the fallen state of humanity. (The order and meaning of each of these lines was later reversed by Christ to become the Lord's Prayer we know today.) The Fall is universal, but healing is always through the individual. On his journey into the old mysteries, therefore, no answer was given to Jesus, only suffering.

The only people who retained some of the purity and spiritual integrity of the past were the Essenes, who lived in communities all over the country. They were disciplined, frugal and intensely active, allowing the adversarial powers no access to them at all. However, demonic powers do not simply disappear if you exclude them from your own life – they simply go elsewhere. This is what Jesus of Nazareth experienced during his years as a trusted lay member of the Essene community. The people outside the closed gates had to suffer the attentions of the banished demonic beings; the goodness of the Essenes became the badness of others. Here, Jesus learned that evil must be transformed, not rejected.

All of this happened in the eighteen years following the scene in the temple. Wherever Jesus looked, he experienced the absence of the living Spirit. This caused him to suffer greatly, even though it was not about him; he burned with the suffering of the world and it became his own suffering: an objective love and compassion for humanity. It is not the intention of this study to describe everything that happened during these eighteen years. That is best done by reading *The Fifth Gospel* itself. The emphasis here is on the disorganising impact this period had on Jesus of Nazareth because he identified so deeply with suffering humanity. Rudolf Steiner relates this to what subsequently took place: 'It is important to realise that the Mystery of Golgotha had to be prepared in this way, with feelings of loneliness and isolation arising in the soul of Jesus of Nazareth.'[10] Jesus began to take on the karma of humanity, but was not yet aware of how it was to be healed.

Here we meet the same gesture as in biological embryology, but in an almost unrecognisably sublime form. The disorder brought about in the cell through the meeting of polarities allows the spirit germ to enter, and thus for something new to begin. In the higher embryology, eighteen years is needed between the meeting of polarities

– the two Jesus children – in the temple scene and the entry of the Christ at the Baptism in the Jordan. In the ordinary embryology, the order that is broken up is also something spiritual – the complex processes within a cell are a working of the etheric in us under the care of the ego-organisation, which 'knows' whose cell it is. It is deeply spiritual, but it has to be partly broken down for a yet greater spirit, the spirit germ, to enter. In the higher embryology, spiritual forces are also at work in Jesus of Nazareth, the thinking, feeling and willing of the Zarathustra and Nathan forces. But all of that had to be broken down if an even higher spirit was to enter earth existence. This breakdown can also be thought of as an offering, an emptying out of what exists to make way for the new. In this state of mind, how did Jesus find his way to John in the River Jordan?

Jesus' conversation with Mary

At this point it is necessary to look at the families in which the boys grew up. Here we find some of the ordered magic that can come about when a great story is being told, an event of deepest significance to the world. Both children lived in Nazareth in Galilee, and both had parents called Mary and Joseph. Both were of the House of David, having a common lineage until that point when, with the sons of King David, the Solomon line and the Nathan line diverged.

Death at a young age was common, and so it happened that Mary, the mother of the Luke child died, as subsequently did Joseph, the father of the Matthew child. These were the two who had received the words from the angel about the child who was to be born, and it was that Mary who kept all things 'in her heart'. They had fulfilled their task of witnessing the Annunciation. It was also common in that time and in that culture for closely connected families to join together when such circumstances arose. So it was that the Matthew Mary became the stepmother of the Luke Jesus, who now also bore the Zarathustra spirit, which had been born in the Matthew Jesus.

In Matthew's Gospel we hear almost nothing of this Mary and so we have less of a picture of who she was. However, there have been artists who painted Mary in different ways. In the *Isenheim Altarpiece* (displayed in Colmar) Grünewald painted a very simple Mary, dressed in the traditional blue and red (see page 74 and inside front cover). The child is wrapped in a ragged cloth, and he is looking at her in adoration. In his hands is a rosary, an image of prayer. In the background there are two shepherds receiving the proclamation from heaven. It is easy to see that this is the Luke story, chosen by the artist for this greatest of altarpieces.

The other painting, also by Grünewald, the *Stuppach Madonna* (or *Madonna in the Garden*) shows us a very different Mary (see page 75 and inside front cover). She is again dressed in blue and red, but in this paining her clothes are richly adorned. She holds what looks like a withered apple – always an image of the Fall – and the child standing on her knee is very alert. The expression on her face is more thoughtful than that of the Colmar Mary who is simply adoring. The heavens are open, and the Father God and many angels are looking down on them. There is no proclamation and there are no shepherds. This is a painting of the Matthew Mary. Again, the polarities between the gospels show themselves, this time in art. There were artists like Grünewald who could sense these things without offending the theological orthodoxy of the time.

There is a story about the birth of the Matthew Mary in the Gospel of James, which is part of the Apocryphal New Testament. It tells us that her parents, Joachim and Anna, were very rich but childless. By the grace of God, however, a daughter was born to them, and in their joy they promised her to the temple in Jerusalem at the age of three, which was often the destiny of special children. Mary grew up a devoted servant and pupil, learning the ways of holiness and the substance of the Judaic religion. She was on the Zarathustra side of the polarity, as the Luke Mary was on the Nathan side.

THE INCARNATION OF CHRIST: A SPIRITUAL EMBRYOLOGY

The simple Mary and Jesus of Luke's Gospel. Detail of Matthias Grünewald's Nativity *in the* Isenheim Altarpiece.

The thoughtful Mary and Jesus of Matthew's Gospel. Detail of Matthias Grünewald's Stuppach Madonna.

It was therefore a defining moment in the life of Jesus of Nazareth when he spoke about his experiences over the last eighteen years to his stepmother, who had grown up and been nurtured in the temple. He poured everything out of himself, a last offering of all his pain at the suffering of humanity. She was ready to receive it. This is the archetype for all healing conversations to this day: one who empties their soul and the other who lovingly hears it. After this was done, it was as if the Zarathustra being who had brought him to this point had fulfilled his destiny and could depart, leaving the pure Nathan being. This was the last step in becoming empty enough for the third stage of the higher conception: the Baptism in the Jordan. Rudolf Steiner says about this:

> Now an impulse arose in the threefold shell [the body, life and soul of Jesus of Nazareth after the departure of Zarathustra]. It drove him to take the road that would lead him to John the Baptist by the River Jordan. He went on his way as though in a dream, yet it was not a dream but a higher state of consciousness ... The threefold shell guided him, and he was scarcely conscious of anything around him.[11]

The remnant of Zarathustra in him allowed him to be aware of the dwindling of the spirit at work in human destiny, and that this was the cause of his suffering. This was what led him to the River Jordan and to John.

The Baptism by John

Baptism by John had a certain direction. When he baptised those who were prepared, they were held under water, almost drowning. In that excarnated state they would be able to perceive their life, and all their errors and deviations from truth. They would see all the ways in which they had made mistakes through being incarnated in an earthly body, which could bring about a distortion of destiny. In returning to the body, they brought with them what they had learned, allowing them to find themselves anew and even change their destiny. With this baptism the emphasis was on excarnation.

The legends that surround John the Baptist describe how he always walked in a straight line, removing obstacles as he came to them rather than finding a way around them. This is what he wanted for those who came to him. His baptism had an upward direction so that in excarnation each person would learn how to straighten their path. However, this is not what happened when Jesus of Nazareth came to John to be baptised. He did not excarnate because he had already created the spiritual space into which something else could incarnate. The Christ spirit was able to enter the unworldly seed of an 'I' that was the being of the Nathan Jesus.

This was a moment of transformation for the whole of humanity. The direction of all spiritual paths for human beings was changed in the moment of the Baptism. The goal was no longer to acquire spiritual experience by going out of oneself, but to find a way that led deeper into oneself, which is much more difficult because one has to meet oneself from within.

From the moment of the Baptism, the higher 'pregnancy' began that ultimately led to the birth of the Resurrection Body. Looking at this alongside the picture of biological conception, we can see certain alignments and similarities. It is not possible to state these as absolute certainties, just to notice that the parallels are there and to compare them.

In biological conception, the meeting of the three necessary elements come together, seemingly simultaneously: the uniting of male and female germ cells, which create the new space for the spirit germ to enter in from an entirely different realm. The earthly substance becomes for one moment able to open to the highest heavens, through the disordering effect of bodily conception. The higher 'I', or individuality, which has passed through all incarnations, has not yet incarnated at this point – only the spirit germ has arrived on earth. These two – the higher 'I' and the sprit germ – belong together, the 'spiritual forces of the physical body' being the expression in form of the 'I', or spirit. So, for example, a human spirit could not incarnate in an animal form. The human being must have just exactly this human form.

The two principles that concern us here, the spirit germ and the higher 'I', belong together although they incarnate at different times. The spirit germ enters at conception, the higher 'I' seventeen to eighteen days later when the sheaths have been formed, for it is into the sheaths, especially the placenta, that it enters. The tiny, hardly there developing embryo could not bear the power of the higher 'I' that already knows so much. That spirit must remain outside in its own realm, near the earth but not yet of the earth. For this reason, the first stages of development are intended to create an earthly place for that karma-carrying individuality. The embryonic sheaths are the first organs to be developed. The embryo, the future body, consists at this time, of two layers of simple cells, which act as an anchor for the developing sheaths. The two that concern us here are the amnion and the placenta.

The amnion is the first to develop, from the top layer (or ectoderm) of the embryo. It will later surround the growing child in the womb with fluid, so that the child floats. The most important, for this study, is the placenta to which the growing child is connected by means of the umbilical cord. This sustains the foetus during pregnancy, providing nutrition and facilitating excretion, breathing and blood circulation. The only thing it doesn't provide are nerves and bone. As the pregnancy progresses, the placenta hands over its forces to the developing child, which then form the heart, liver, lungs, digestive tract, and so on. Only when this has been completed can the placenta be discarded. This is birth, the first stage of independent existence on earth. But the placenta does much more than provide the forces for a living body. The placenta is also the organ into which the higher 'I' incarnates, and which can then ray into the embryo. It is very individual, we can say karmic, how much the higher 'I' works into the developmental processes, and how much is done through hereditary forces (DNA can manage very well on its own). On the whole there is an interplay between these two, between the past and the future, for the higher 'I' always brings something new, and genetics is primarily of the past.

The placenta has always been seen as a sacred organ. During pregnancy the higher 'I' of the child is nearer than it will ever naturally be, for it has incarnated into a physical organ, and has its influence on the child from there.

Looking at this from a Christological perspective we see something of the same, but with very important differences. When Christ incarnated into the Nathan Jesus at the Baptism in the Jordan, the higher conception was enabled. Unlike biological conception, there was no need to separate any spirit germ from the spirit itself. The spirit germ, the essence of the human form, was already there in the being of the Nathan Jesus who had a body through the Nathan line. He also had in its purest form the never-before incarnated 'I'. This 'I' had not experienced the Fall and had served Christ in the spiritual world to create a form that possessed the purely human characteristics of uprightness, speech and thought. Together with all that had happened to him on the earth, the Nathan Jesus became the body into which Christ could directly incarnate.

In the biological embryology, the spirit is kept separate from the developing body and influences it from the placenta. The higher spirit cannot be integrated with earthly substance without causing harm both through its intensity and through the individual karma that it bears. Christ had no karma and so he could enter directly into the body of the Nathan Jesus. In that sense he was the spirit-bearing placenta carrying the forces to develop a new body, the Resurrection Body. Christ prepared his future incarnation in the spiritual world. Because of this the Nathan Jesus could sustain a being as powerful as Christ. He prepared a form that is archetypal for all human beings, but made it specific to himself in order to be able to live on earth.

In *The Fifth Gospel,* Steiner described that when Jesus of Nazareth was thirty the Zarathustra 'I' departed, making a space for the Christ to enter at the Baptism in the Jordan. This was the greatest offering that Zarathustra made: to 'die' at this point without meeting Christ himself. He gave the greatest help towards this event, but did not himself experience its centre point on earth. He did not meet Christ.

The Two Embryologies

The essential difference between the two embryologies
The two embryologies are the reverse of each other in every respect.

Biological embryology begins with the physical. In fact, the earliest form, the ball of cells called the morula, is so tough that it can be frozen and used for in vitro fertilisation. One can think of that as a property of the material world. It then develops the sheaths, the two layers of the embryo becoming three, and from this, through growth and metamorphosis, all the organs needed for independent life develop. The complexity of development in both form and function make it possible for an individual soul and, ultimately, spirit to have a home in physical substance. After the placenta has been discarded at birth, the higher spirit that dwelt within it can only be consciously taken hold of during the course of that person's life. Each one of us is free to do this or not. The full extent of the incarnation of the spirit is given in the Pentecost story (Acts 2) when the Holy Spirit was bestowed on the disciples. In biological embryology, the direction of development is from the physical to the soul-spiritual.

Christological embryology, however, begins with the being of Christ entering the adult body of Jesus at the Baptism. Jesus's physical body was then transformed during the following three years, resulting in the birth of the Resurrection Body on Easter Sunday, a spiritual body of the kind that had never before existed on earth. In this sense it is the reverse of biological embryology, which develops a physical body to become a home for the invisible, incarnated spirit.

This is an important point. Both embryologies create a body, the first being earthly, the second spiritual, although the latter was perceptible to those who could see him. Both bodies breathe. In John 20, we hear how the Resurrected One appeared on the first day of the week, Easter Sunday, showed himself to the disciples and said, 'Peace be with you. As the Father has sent me, so I send you.' And then he breathed on them and said, 'Receive the Holy Spirit.' He breathed out something life-giving. The carbon dioxide we normally breathe out is poison for the earth, but it is redeemed by plants which breathe it in. The Risen Christ, however, had a very different physiology to our earthly one. As well as breathing out a life-giving spirit, he asked

Thomas to touch him. He used physical means to show that his body was beyond matter but nonetheless perceptible to the sense of touch, the most earthly of all the senses. This is the heart of the mystery.

The Resurrection Body

Rudolf Steiner said very little about the Resurrection Body. He said much that was relevant to it, but he allowed the transformation of Jesus's body to remain a mystery. Indeed, he said:

> If the Mystery of Golgotha were to be comprehensible to human reasoning [with the thinking of today] ... then there would have been no need for it to take place.[12]

It can only be approached with the greatest reverence and humility, and with certain possibilities of thought that do not necessarily join up to create a whole picture.

The anchor point of this study is the quotation from *The Fifth Gospel,* stating that the three years of Christ's life within Jesus can be likened to the nine months in the womb in biological embryology. From this perspective something can be learned about the Resurrection. The embryological approach becomes a way to approach the mystery. Though the Christological process is the reverse of the biological one, and takes place over a longer period of time, there are nonetheless strong parallels between the two.

In both there is a conception involving the archetypal meeting of male and female – either in the meeting of cells, or in the event in the temple when the 'male' element of the Matthew Jesus united with the more 'female' element of the Luke Jesus. Both conceptions are graced with a third element, the spirit germ in the biological, and the Christ spirit that incarnates in Jesus of Nazareth in the other. Both of these elements are made possible by the destruction of order – one could even say, rather bluntly, that this is the inherent task of the male–female polarity. In biological embryology it is the destabilising of substance within the cell, a potentially dangerous situation. In the Christological embryology it is the destabilising experiences of Jesus of Nazareth during the eighteen years between the scene in the temple and the Baptism that creates the space for the Christ spirit to enter in. Even the time difference between the instantaneous entry of the spirit germ and the eighteen years in the Jesus biography can be seen to have the same dynamic of allowing the highest to enter the earthly.

The process of identification and the Resurrection

The higher embryology begins with the spirit, which must then transform the astral, etheric and physical bodies of Jesus during the three years so that the Resurrection Body can be born. The death of Jesus on the cross is essential to this transformative process. How did the resurrection of all the organs and their participation in body, soul and spirit take place? How did he walk among people for forty days after the Resurrection until the Ascension? What kind of body could do that? It is possible to find threads of an answer, although they cannot yet be joined into a coherent whole. The first approach to this comes in *The Fifth Gospel:*

> Initially [after the Baptism] the Christ spirit was relatively independent of the living body of Jesus of Nazareth, but as time went on it had to adapt to it more and more. As life progressed it was increasingly bound to the body of Jesus of Nazareth, and in the final year it caused the Christ spirit immense pain to be bound to this body, which had also grown frail.[13]

Once again, there is the theme of pain and suffering as a transformative necessity. Over the course of the three years Christ identified more and more with the body of Jesus of Nazareth, Christ and Jesus became ever closer. What does this mean? It is natural for us to identify with our bodies; that is what it means to be incarnated on the earth: where I am, there is my body. We experience our 'I' within our body during our waking hours, and even when we are asleep, the relationship between our 'I' and body is maintained by the thread of life. But we do not have as complete an identification with our bodies and all its organs as we think.

If that were so, then with our 'I' we would be able to govern all the processes within our bodies in full consciousness. We would be able to master everything that, for instance, the liver is doing at every moment. The liver is one of the most complex and busiest organs in the body and we are completely unconscious of its activities. Indeed, much that goes on in our bodies has to be given over to nature and the beings that work incessantly in nature in us. Our individuality is present in these processes – it is *my* liver, so to speak, not just a general one – but it is unconscious. The myriad biochemical processes that occur in us are not at our command: we are not 'at one' with all aspects of ourselves or conscious of each cell in our bodies.

The only time in the whole cycle of life and death when we are in total communion with ourselves is at the

Midnight Hour of existence, when we are as far away spiritually from the earth as it is possible to be – and even there we need the help of high spiritual beings to sustain us. At this midpoint between incarnations, the 'I' has expanded to the dimensions of the cosmos and is able to unite with the zodiacal realms that are the archetypes of the body. 'I' and body, the image of zodiac, become one, and out of that communion the spirit germ for the next earthly body is formed. Only there is our consciousness able to grasp every element of the human form, and we become a participant in the forming of each organ from within that organ. Rudolf Steiner gave an example of this:

> If you survey what lies in a single pulmonary vesicle, it will appear more grandiose than the whole range of the mighty Alps. For what lies inside of man is the whole spiritual cosmos in condensed form.[14]

The intention of the spiritual world is that this conscious communion should also be present on earth in human form.

With this in mind, perhaps it is possible to imagine that the identification of Christ's being with Jesus of Nazareth was creative in the same way that the communion of 'I' and zodiac is for each of us at the Midnight Hour. And that this communion brought about the tender beginnings of a new body – the Resurrection Body – in which each part, each cell, possessed 'I'-consciousness: the bones as conscious as the head. This moment in earthly life could be called the Midday Hour. The impression from the Gospel of John (20:17) – 'Do not hold me, for I have not yet ascended to the Father' – is that this took time to form. It is a process.

This is something new in the cosmos, that there can be bodily substance, the blood for example, wherein every cell has Christ consciousness, has been Christ-ened. It presents the possibility that there can be a bodily form that is more than the creation of the spirit germ in cooperation with heredity and individuality. Through the Resurrection this can also be a Christ-conscious form. The form of the spirit germ is cosmic, for we have all had to become cosmic in form in order to find the creative communion that is necessary to create the body in the next life. The Resurrection Body, however, has the human form as we know it on the earth, not the form of the cosmos. It is at one and the same time cosmic and earthly. One can have a fleeting glimpse of this by looking at two of the Raphael cartoons in the Victoria and Albert Museum in London. In *The Miraculous Draught of Fishes,* the Christ who is incarnated in Jesus of Nazareth is solidly there, communicating with his disciples in a recognisably earthly way. In *Christ's Charge to Peter,* the resurrected Christ, who is beyond incarnation or excarnation, has a tender, almost transparent presence (see pages 92f and inside back cover).

It is important to emphasise the difference between these two kinds of communion, the one at the Midnight Hour and Christ's communion with Jesus of Nazareth. To achieve the first, each human being must expand after death to the dimensions of the cosmos. The spirit germ is not what we would recognise as the human form, with torso, limbs, head and all the inner organs. It is round but dimensionless, and it can be created only because the human 'I' is able to encompass the dimensions of the zodiac. On earth we experience ourselves as 'I' at the centre looking outwards, but the 'I' must expand to the periphery without losing its I-ness if the spirit germ is to be created.

During the journey towards a new incarnation, this seed form must cooperate after conception with the biological and earthly forces. The result is the form that we all recognise as the physical body. It is a very accurate process, with few mistakes compared to the imperfections of the more conscious soul and spirit, which are like infants compared to the perfection of the physical body. In us the 'I' is conscious only in the head and unconscious in the rest of us. In the Christological communion, however, the

*The incarnated Christ.
Detail from Raphael's* The Miraculous Draught of Fishes.

Christ 'I' took his shining power into each cell of the body of Jesus of Nazareth. Each cell became as conscious as the head and could therefore create something new: a body in human form with the perfection of the spirit germ.

In this new event the periphery has become centre and this makes the human form divine. This is as true for the

THE TWO EMBRYOLOGIES

*The resurrected Christ.
Detail from Raphael's* Christ's Charge to Peter.

spiritual world as it is for the earth; all is entirely new. This relationship of centre and periphery as it reveals itself in spirit germ and Resurrection Body is central to this study, and has been repeated in various ways because it is so fundamental and not easy to grasp. The challenge is to think centre and periphery at the same time.

It is one embryology, not two

Until now, this study has described two forms of embryology. There is the biological one that is an essential part of the biography of each one of us. We have all been conceived as earthly human beings, and each one of us must find a balance between what heredity has given to us and what we have brought with us from the spiritual world as individual karma and our life's task. These two streams in us have to be able to speak to each other, and adapt to each other, both biologically and spiritually.

The second is the Christological one, which has occurred only once on earth. Certain children had to be born so that Christ would have the necessary basis for his incarnation on earth. The embryological motif shows itself in the scene in the temple when the 'I' of the Matthew Jesus child unites with the 'I' of the Luke Jesus child. This is equivalent to the merging of the male and female polarities in biological conception, only on a higher level. In both forms of conception, a place is created for the spirit to enter in: in the biological form, the spirit germ; in the higher conception, the Christ being – the 'I' of humanity – at the Baptism. In both cases a new body is formed. There is a great deal of knowledge about how the physical body is formed, but almost nothing about the Resurrection

Body. Some hints have been suggested as to how this may have happened, but no more than a whisper, for that is the mystery of this earth.

We can, however, see them as one embryology, with human beings fulfilling the biological side and only Christ able to fulfil the spiritual side. These two may appear separate, but there is an aspect of human existence in which they overlap, and that is the human 'I' – embedded in human biological development, but capable of being spiritually inspired, even Christ-inspired.

On the whole, we are not free in the biological part of our biography: there are processes of growth and metamorphosis that follow natural law and what is encoded in our DNA. However, the spiritual individuality can work its way into this, and if that individuality is strong enough, and if biography allows it, it is possible to transcend natural and even karmic laws. Then one's own spiritual path can be found. The higher 'I', which is present in the placenta throughout pregnancy, excarnates when the child is born and is found again only by individual effort during our life on earth. Through this effort we can spiritually place a foot on the second embryological path. In any one lifetime it is possible to take some small, faltering steps towards resurrection. Only Christ, who carried no personal karma, could fulfil this in its entirety, and only when the conditions had been carefully prepared through long ages of time and with the participation of the whole cosmos.

The ultimate destiny of every human being is to reach as far as a resurrection body. The time that is spent on earth as a gift of biological embryology is vital to any further development, for it is here that deeds can be done and be imprinted onto the life after death. Only there can those deeds be truly understood and therefore inform future intentions. As a general rule, on earth we *do* things, after death we *understand* them. It is during the time on earth that the bridge between the two embryologies can be discovered.

Birth in the Gospel of John

The connection between the two embryologies is to be found in the 'birth' story in the John Gospel, which tells of the eternal birth of the Word, from which all things are created. Human beings have access to this eternal creativity through our 'I'. In normal, everyday life, this is the word we use to refer to ourselves and it is used liberally in almost everything we say: 'I think this ...', 'I did this ...', 'I am going there ...' and so on. The 'I' has become identified with everything that is thought, felt or done because everything that the soul experiences has become 'I'. This is an evolutionary necessity if human beings are to be truly on the earth. Human evolution has progressed so far that consciousness is now confined to the sense world, and only through our bodily existence do we experience an 'I'. This 'I' is earthbound and prone to error. Christ came to earth to spiritualise this body-bound 'I', to Christ-en it. This is a new step in the evolution of human beings and of the universe.

However, the 'I' can be experienced for itself apart from everything that is thought, done or felt. When this happens, either spontaneously or through spiritual exercises that aim to bring this about, a whole new world opens up to us. The essence of this is to be found in the seven 'I am' sayings in the Gospel of John. They are not present in any other gospel and they express what the 'I am' is in itself. They are experience, not thought. The 'I am' is the experience of being nourished: 'I am the bread of life' (6:35), the food which connects the earthly with the heavenly. It is also the means by which everything can be illuminated and understood: 'I am the light of the world' (8:12). All the knowledge painstakingly gained through the senses finds its meaning through these words of Christ, the embodiment of the 'I am'. The safe passage from one realm to another, from earthly to spiritual comes through him. The 'I am' is the door (10:7), a threshold that can be opened or closed by the 'I am' as the Good Shepherd (10:11). The 'I am' is the seed of resurrection, and the death that must proceed it: 'I am the resurrection and the life' (11:25). It is also the way, the truth and the life (14:6), and the very core of being: 'I am the true vine' (15:1).

The seven 'I am' sayings are not separate from each other; they are distinguishable but not separate. The nourishment is at the same time the way, the core of being, and the seed of resurrection. There is an image of this in the gospels, when the soldiers at Jesus Christ's crucifixion divide his clothes among them. His tunic has no seams and cannot be divided, and so rather than tear it up, the soldiers cast lots to see who will win it (19:23–24). The higher 'I' does indeed have to be won; it is very rarely just 'given'. In the gospels this raised form of the 'I' is called the Holy Spirit, also the Comforter or Healing Spirit, because the experience of this alleviates all pain and earthly troubles. It is the source of true forgiveness, which cannot be willed but is given as part of the wholeness of the Comforter. The experience ultimately is one of grace. In anthroposophy this is called the spirit self, the spiritualised 'I' that can transcend its field of activity beyond the sense world. Yet it is built upon the 'I' that all human beings develop in the natural course of their lifetimes. The 'I' is turned towards mastering the sense world, but it has within it the power to turn the forces of the soul towards a higher form of itself, and it can prepare for that. Its very freedom lies in its ability to choose to do this, or not.

It is around this point, the 'I' point, that the bridge can be built between the two embryologies, and there are as many forms of this bridge as there are human beings. Each person has their own heredity, destiny and individual biography, but each person can take a step towards the Christ embryology, for that is universal and belongs to all.

Conclusion

The word 'embryology' derives from the Greek *en bruon*, meaning to grow, to sprout and develop within. That is why the title of this study emphasises the embryological aspect of both human and spiritual, Christological, development. The two were connected by Rudolf Steiner when he stated that the three years of Christ's existence on earth can be likened to the nine months of pregnancy in the human being, both resulting in a body.

It has been shown that these two have certain gestures in common, perhaps we could even call them laws. In both, for the highest spirit to incarnate, earthly laws must be brought into disorder. To bring this about, the polarity of male and female was created. In the biological, that is the development of the germ cells, in the Christological, the two Jesus boys. By assigning gender to the polarities we found in the birth stories, and emphasising the same polarities in the biological process, it has been possible to bring the two realms together. The uniting of the polarities at both levels of conception shakes up the natural as well as the soul-spiritual order. This is an opening that allows the higher spirit to enter. In biological embryology that occurs first of all with the spirit germ and then about eighteen days later with the higher 'I', which works into the embryo from the placenta. One can say that the cell 'suffers', as Jesus suffered in the eighteen years after the event in the temple. Only through that could the being of Christ enter earthly substance.

Cosmic laws are at work here, whether that is conferring spiritual individuality to each human being's earthly embodiment, or raising up a unique embodiment to cosmic existence.

Notes

1. *The Fifth Gospel,* lecture of Oct 3, 1913, p. 31.
2. *Philosophy, Cosmology and Religion,* lecture of Sep 11, 1922, p. 90.
3. *Man's Being, his Destiny and World Evolution,* lecture of 17 May 1923, pp. 23, 32.
4. *Cosmic Memory,* Ch. 6, pp. 87.
5. *The Reappearance of Christ in the Etheric,* lecture of March 5, 1910, pp. 65f.
6. *According to Luke,* lecture 4, Sep 18, 1909, p. 93.
7. *Approaching the Mystery of Golgotha.* lecture of March 7, 1914, p. 85.
8. *Life of the Human Soul,* lecture of May 27, 1922.
9. *According to Luke,* lecture 7, Sep 21, 1909, p. 141.
10. *The Fifth Gospel,* lecture of Dec 17. 1913, p. 193.
11. *The Fifth Gospel,* lecture of Dec 17. 1913, pp. 203f.
12. *The World of the Senses,* lecture of Dec 29, 1911, p. 43.
13. *The Fifth Gospel,* lecture of Oct 6, 1913, p. 81.
14. *Man's Being, his Destiny and World Evolution,* lecture of 17 May 1923, p. 25.

Bibliography

Langman, Jan, and T.W. Sadler, *Medical Embryology,* Lippincott Williams & Wilkins, USA 1997.

Steiner, Rudolf. Volume Nos refer to the Collected Works (CW).

—, *According to Luke* (CW 114) Anthroposophic Press, USA 2001 (tr. Catherine Creeger).

—, *According to Matthew* (CW 123) Anthroposophic Press, USA 2003 (tr. Catherine Creeger).

—, *Approaching the Mystery of Golgotha* (CW 152) SteinerBooks, USA 2006 (tr. Michael Miller).

—, *Aus der Akasha-Forschung: Das fünfte Evangelium* (GA 148) Rudolf Steiner Verlag, Switzerland 1992.

—, *Cosmic Memory* (CW 11) SteinerBooks, USA 2020.

—, *The Fifth Gospel: From the Akashic Record* (CW 148) Rudolf Steiner Press, UK 2014 (tr. A.R. Meeus).

—, *Life of the Human Soul and its Relation to World Evolution* (CW 212) Rudolf Steiner Press, UK 2016 (tr. Matthew Barton).

—, *Man's Being, his Destiny and World Evolution* (CW 226) Anthroposophic Press, USA 1984 (tr. Erna McArthur).

—, *Philosophy, Cosmology and Religion* (CW 215) Anthroposophic Press, USA 1984 (tr. Lisa Monges & Doris Bugbey).

—, 'The Pre-Earthly Deeds of Christ,' lecture of March 7, 1914 in *Approaching the Mystery of Golgotha.*

—, *The Reappearance of Christ in the Etheric* (CW 118) SteinerBooks, USA 2003.

—, *The World of the Senses and the World of the Spirit* (CW 134) Rudolf Steiner Press, UK 1995 (tr. Johanna Collis).

Acknowledgements

My thanks go to Sophia Smith and Jeremy Smith, who encouraged and accompanied me throughout writing. To Tom Ravetz and Antoinette Reynolds, for reading the text so positively. To Peter Selg for his interest which led to the German edition of this book and the Foreword, and to Christian Maclean for all the helpful editing.

Figures

All line drawings are by the author. Art pictures from Wiki Commons.

For news on all our **latest books**,
and to receive **exclusive discounts**,
join our mailing list at:

florisbooks.co.uk/signup

Plus subscribers get a FREE book
with every online order!

We will never pass your details to anyone else.

www.ingramcontent.com/pod-product-compliance
Lightning Source LLC
Chambersburg PA
CBHW061213070526
44583CB00025B/3230